Steven
SPIELBERG

Steven SPIELBERG

Tom Powers

A&E.

Lerner Publications Company
Minneapolis

For my mother

A&E and **BIOGRAPHY** are trademarks of the A&E Television Networks, registered in the United States and other countries.

Some of the people profiled in this series have also been featured in A&E's acclaimed BIOGRAPHY series, which is available on videocassette from A&E Home Video. Call 1-800-423-1212 to order.

First Avenue Editions
A division of Lerner Publishing Group
241 First Avenue North
Minneapolis, MN 55401 U.S.A.

Website address: www.lernerbooks.com

Library of Congress Cataloging-in-Publication Data

Powers, Tom (Tom J.)
    Steven Spielberg / by Tom Powers.
        p. cm. — (A&E biography)
    "Originally published in 1997 by Lerner Publications Company under the title Steven Spielberg : master storyteller."
    Includes bibliographical references and index.
    ISBN 0-8225-9694-6 (pbk. : alk. paper)
    1. Spielberg, Steven, 1947– Juvenile literature. 2. Motion picture producers and directors—United States—Biography—Juvenile literature.
[1. Spielberg, Steven, 1947– 2. Motion picture producers and directors.] I. Title. II. Series.
PN1998.3.S65 P68 2000
791.43'0233'092—dc21   00-010281

Manufactured in the United States of America
1 2 3 4 5 6 – JR – 05 04 03 02 01 00

CONTENTS

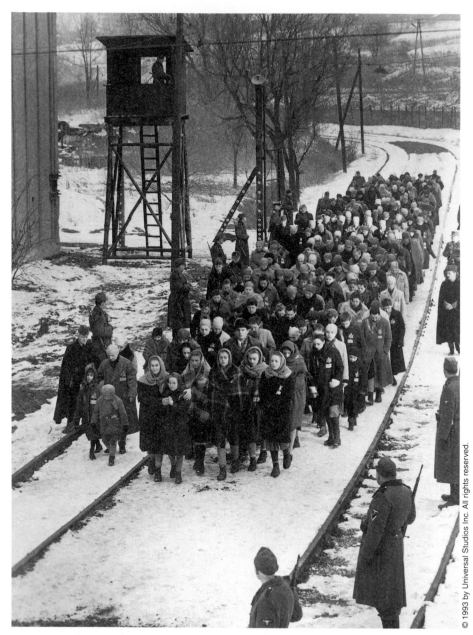

Schindler's List *was a personal and professional triumph for Steven Spielberg.*

INTRODUCTION

A SIGN HANGS ACROSS THE ENTRANCE TO THE camp. *ARBEIT MACHT FREI*, the sign reads in German. "Work will make you free." The sign is a lie. Nobody ever worked their way out of this place. This is Auschwitz, a death camp. More than one million people were murdered here.

In October 1944, a train chugged through the countryside of southern Poland, pulling a load of cattle cars. As the train approached Auschwitz, its brakes screeched. The powerful, surging engine began to slow. When the train reached the outer yard of the camp, surrounded by thick walls and barbed-wire fences, it came to a halt.

Spotlights were aimed at the train from tall guard towers. Dogs held tightly on leashes snarled and barked at the figures in the cattle cars. The dogs' breath hung like white steam in the chilly night air. Soldiers wearing heavy overcoats stood with their rifles slung over their shoulders. Next to them stood prisoners wearing striped uniforms.

As soon as the train stopped, the prisoners moved forward. They flung open the boxcar doors and raised wooden gangplanks to the cars. The boxcars were packed tightly—not with cattle, but with women. The women wore thin coats or no coats at all. Their heads were wrapped in scarves and their eyes were huge with fear. The women were Polish Jews who had been brought to Auschwitz to be killed.

The women jumped down onto the gangplanks, then ran across the snow-covered yard. Guards herded the women toward a low door in a huge brick building. "*Schnell, schnell,*" the guards cried. "Quickly, quickly."

High atop the building, a giant smokestack belched flame and ash into the night sky. The ash fluttered down to the ground softly, like a memory. It was all that was left of the people who had been murdered and incinerated this day inside this building, inside this death camp.

Then a voice pierced the night and everything stopped and everything changed. "Cut!" yelled the voice. Suddenly the year was not 1944, but 1992. The women and the soldiers and the prisoners and the snarling dogs were only actors in a movie. The spotlights were movie lights. A camera moved through the air on a small crane. Production assistants brought blankets and cups of coffee to shivering actors. The movie's director talked with the cameraman about filming the next scene.

The movie was *Schindler's List.* It told the story of a group of Jews who survived the death camps of World War II. In the early 1940s, the Nazi government of Germany made a plan to kill all the Jews in Europe. The Nazis hated and feared Jews. Jewish men, women, and children were brought to concentration camps like Auschwitz, where they were starved, worked to death, shot, or gassed. Then their bodies were burned. The Nazis killed six million Jews and millions of other people in a slaughter that came to be known as the Holocaust. "Holocaust" means the destruction of people or animals by fire.

The director of *Schindler's List* was Steven Spielberg. Spielberg is Jewish, and in making a film about the Holocaust, he felt a strong sense of responsibility. Millions of Jews around the world were counting on him to do honor to the memory of the dead. Spielberg had not always followed his religion devoutly, but he said that when he came to Poland to make his movie, "Jewish life came pouring back into my heart." Some of Spielberg's own ancestors came from the part of Poland where he filmed *Schindler's List.*

Spielberg was the most popular and financially successful filmmaker of all time. His films included *Jaws, E.T. The Extra-Terrestrial, Raiders of the Lost Ark,* and *Close Encounters of the Third Kind.* Spielberg made beautifully crafted films. Audiences and critics alike praised his films for their powerful acting, careful lighting, and dazzling special effects.

But in a way, no one took Spielberg seriously. His movies made money—lots of money—but they did not win awards, and they did not gain Spielberg the respect he wanted. Spielberg made great movies, people said, but they were "kids' movies," movies about killer sharks and flying saucers and a whip-snapping action hero named

Indiana Jones. Even as he filmed *Schindler's List,* Spielberg was editing another "kids' movie"—one about rampaging dinosaurs.

Not everyone believed that Steven Spielberg should make *Schindler's List.* Many people doubted that Spielberg could make a "serious" film, as a movie about the Holocaust would have to be. Spielberg asked for permission to film some scenes for *Schindler's List* inside Auschwitz. (The camp still stands in Poland, as a reminder of the Holocaust.) Nine other movie crews had been given permission to film inside the camp. Spielberg's request, however, was denied. The director was told that the camp was a holy place, a memorial to those who had died there. It was suggested that Spielberg was not a serious enough director to work inside Auschwitz.

> **M**ANY PEOPLE DOUBTED THAT SPIELBERG COULD MAKE A "SERIOUS" FILM, AS A MOVIE ABOUT THE HOLOCAUST WOULD HAVE TO BE.

Spielberg himself admitted that he had never wanted to make movies about pain and suffering. "I've often protected myself with the movie camera," Spielberg said. "The camera has always been my golden shield against things really reaching me."

To make *Schindler's List,* Spielberg had to look deep inside himself. Was he a serious filmmaker? In the past he had made movies about escapes and fantasies and adventures, about brave children and foolish parents. Could he deal with the horrible reality of the Holocaust? To make *Schindler's List,* Spielberg had to draw on all the skills he

Spielberg said that making Schindler's List *brought him back in touch with his identity as a Jew.*

had learned during twenty years as a filmmaker. He also had to examine his own conscience. He had to look at the things he feared and at the things he loved and valued most.

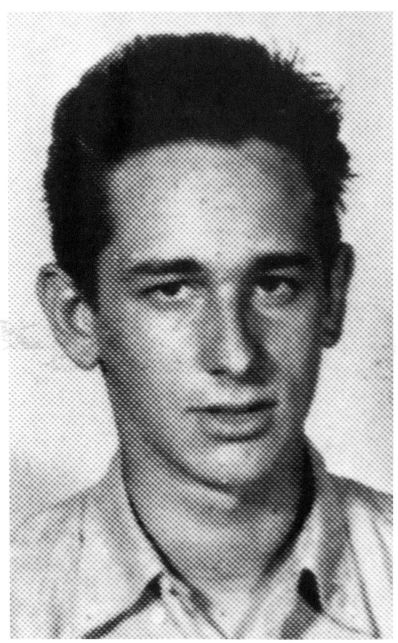

Spielberg in his junior year of high school

THE WEIRD SKINNY KID

STEVEN SPIELBERG MADE HIS FIRST MOVIE ABOUT fighting Nazis when he was thirteen years old. Steven filmed it with a small, 8-millimeter camera that his mother had given his father for Father's Day.

The star of *Battle Squad* was a large boy who liked to beat up Steven and let the air out of his bicycle tires. Steven had nightmares about the bully. He decided that if he could not fight the boy, he would try to win him over.

Steven told the bully that he was making a film about soldiers fighting the Nazis in World War II, and he wanted him to play the hero. The boy laughed in Spielberg's face. Steven was persistent, however, and finally the bully agreed. Steven dressed his new fourteen-year-old star in a helmet, backpack, and military fatigues, trying to make him look like movie star John Wayne. By the time they finished shooting *Battle Squad,* the former bully had become Spielberg's best friend.

From the age of thirteen on, Spielberg knew that he wanted to be a filmmaker. He realized that the movie camera could be his "golden shield," his protection against bullies at school, against trouble at home, against every fear, real or imagined.

Steven Spielberg was born December 18, 1946, in Cincinnati, Ohio, the oldest of four children born to Arnold and Leah Spielberg. Because his father's job required frequent moves, Steven grew up in several places: Cincinnati; Haddonfield, New Jersey; Scottsdale, Arizona; and Saratoga, California. It seemed to Steven that every time he got comfortable with a new town, his family moved someplace else.

Steven's father was an electrical engineer who helped design the first computers. Arnold Spielberg shared his love of science and astronomy with his son, hoping Steven would pursue a career in science. Once, when Steven was six years old, his father woke him up late at night. Together they drove into the countryside to watch a meteor shower. Steven cherished that moment.

Arnold Spielberg encouraged his son to work hard at his math and science classes. Steven, however, was more inclined to follow in his mother's footsteps. From his father Spielberg inherited a love of science fiction, but not the desire to become a scientist.

His mother is probably the person who influenced Steven to become an artist. Leah Spielberg was trained as a classical pianist. She often invited other female musicians to come to the house and play classical music.

Above: *Spielberg with his father, Arnold.*
Left: *Spielberg with his mother, Leah Adler, and his sister Sue*

Steven's father was frequently away on business. "I was raised in a world of women," Spielberg said. "Even the dog was female."

Spielberg's father had little interest in classical music. His passion was computers, and he spent long hours at his job. Leah Spielberg was much more carefree and playful than her husband. Over the years, Arnold and Leah Spielberg grew apart. They had few interests in common. Only their love for their children held the marriage together. As an adult looking back on his childhood, Steven praised his parents for doing such a good job raising him and his sisters even as their marriage was failing.

Besides their oldest child, Steven, the Spielbergs had three daughters, Sue, Anne, and Nancy. Steven loved to torment his sisters. Once he locked them inside a closet, where he had rigged a ghostly skeleton with a light glowing in its eye socket. Another time, he cut off the head of his sister Nancy's favorite doll. Then he placed it on a bed of lettuce, surrounded it with tomato slices, and served it to her on a platter. Steven himself was frightened by dark closets and spooky trees and bathtubs with feet. He learned, however, that he could overcome his own fears by making his sisters even more frightened than he was.

As a boy, Steven was enchanted by movies and television. To make sure that his son was not watching too much television, Arnold Spielberg placed a hair over the television power switch. Steven always found the hair, removed it carefully, then replaced it in the same position when he finished watching television.

Walt Disney films were Steven's favorites, and Disney probably influenced Spielberg more than any other film-maker. Spielberg has said that he was more frightened by the "Night on Bald Mountain" sequence in *Fantasia* than by anything else he ever saw in the movies.

A lot of other things frightened Steven when he was a little boy. A television documentary on snakes made him cry. The death of Bambi's mother left him shaken. When the wicked queen in Disney's *Snow White* turned into a skeleton and crumbled into pieces, Steven covered his eyes and burst into tears. He was even afraid of the dark. "The first scary thing I learned to do as a child," he said, "was turn off the light!"

Spielberg did not give in to his fears, though. He may have gone to bed afraid, but he woke up brave. "In the morning I was the bravest guy—there was little seven-year-old Steven walking around the closet, saying 'I'm not afraid of you.' Or talking to the trees and clouds, saying 'I'm not afraid of you.' But once night fell, all bets were off."

Years later, Spielberg made use of his childhood fears in directing his movies. Most of his films contain power-ful, scary figures: a killer truck, a giant shark, a raging for-est fire, wicked pirates, evil Nazis. Spielberg shares his fears with audiences. "I like to feel my skin crawling un-der my shirt trying to get up to my jugular vein," he said. "I'm diabolical in that sense. I get perverse pleasure in making people sweat in their underwear. It doesn't make me the nicest guy in the world but I sure enjoy it."

Always, however, there is a "little guy" in Spielberg's films who triumphs over fear and evil. Sometimes the "little guy" is an ordinary man or woman. Sometimes it is a child, a boy or girl who must conquer fear and take action, just like young Steven Spielberg.

Steven spent the greatest part of his childhood in Scottsdale, Arizona, a suburb of Phoenix. In school, other students thought Spielberg was a "wimp." "I was the weird skinny kid with acne," he says. He was poor at sports and games. When he was told to dissect a frog in biology class, he threw up. Steven's father allowed him to

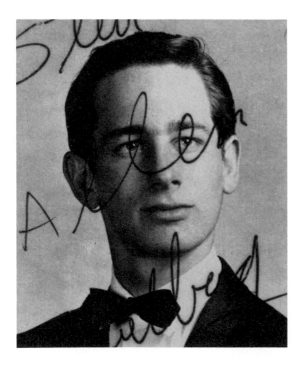

Spielberg's senior year photograph, signed by him

start making family movies because he wanted his son to become more self-confident.

Steven soon took over the house with his moviemaking. He turned the family living room into a movie studio, strewn with electrical cables and floodlights. He overwhelmed the other family members with his eagerness to make movies. According to Spielberg's mother, her son did not understand the meaning of the word *no.*

STEVEN TURNED THE FAMILY LIVING ROOM INTO A MOVIE STUDIO, STREWN WITH ELECTRICAL CABLES AND FLOODLIGHTS.

Spielberg recruited his mother and sisters and friends to act in his films. Spielberg's mother was happy to contribute. She helped him make costumes for his films. She drove him into the Arizona desert when he wanted to film "on location." She exploded thirty cans of cherries in a pressure cooker so that he could film the blood-red glop for scary special effects. Spielberg has said that his mother was like a "big kid," full of fun and enthusiasm for his projects.

At Arcadia High School in Phoenix, Steven joined the theater arts program. He discovered that there were options besides being a popular athlete or a weird skinny kid. When he was fifteen, he made his most ambitious film, a two-and-a-half-hour science fiction epic called *Firelight.* The film cost five hundred dollars and took a year to make, mainly because Steven could only film on weekends. To raise money for the film, he worked after school whitewashing citrus trees (to protect them from insects). When *Firelight* was finished, Steven persuaded a Phoenix movie theater owner to let him show it. The film's "world premiere" took place on March 24, 1963. Spielberg charged admission and ended up making fifty dollars more than the film had cost him.

Shortly after his triumph with *Firelight,* Steven's family moved from Phoenix to Saratoga, California, a suburb of San Jose. There, for the first time, Spielberg felt the sting of prejudice. Spielberg grew up with a strong awareness of his Jewish heritage. His parents and grandparents were often visited by friends and relatives who had survived the Holocaust in Germany. Some of these people had numbers tatooed on their arms—identification marks given to Jews in the concentration camps. Recalling his grandparents' friends, Spielberg said, "I remember when I was three years old learning to count by touching the numbers on the forearm of one of them."

In Arizona, Steven's classmates made fun of him because he was "weird," not because he was Jewish. It was only in his last years of high school that Spielberg was treated badly because of his religion. In study hall, classmates threw pennies at him. Other students called him anti-Semitic names and tried to beat him up.

While Steven was in high school, the Spielberg family was going through a crisis. Soon after they moved to California, Arnold and Leah Spielberg divorced. Steven Spielberg has said that for him *divorce* was the ugliest word in the English language. He and his sisters held each other and cried when they heard their parents arguing and talking about divorce.

Spielberg has called his childhood "semi-unhappy." There were too many moves, too many arguments between his serious father and his fun-loving mother. Spielberg said that the tension between his parents was "not violence, just a pervading unhappiness you could cut with a fork or a spoon at dinner every night." His response was to lose himself in films and television and to make his own movies. For him, movies were a kind of "wishful thinking," a place where he could experience the kind of warm family life that was too often missing in his own childhood.

Although Spielberg grew up in the turbulent 1960s, he was not a rebellious teenager. He did not become a hippie or protest against the war in Vietnam. Later, when he became a filmmaker, Spielberg did not try to question or challenge the values of his audience. According to the critic Robert Kolker, Spielberg's films are basically "conservative." Rather than trying to change how people think or feel, Spielberg makes viewers feel good about the way things are. His films present values that the American audience already accepts, such as the importance of family.

Spielberg shares the values of his audience. His ability to identify with the fears, hopes, and dreams of "everyday people" has made Steven Spielberg the most popular filmmaker of all time.

CHAPTER TWO

"DO YOU WANT TO GO TO COLLEGE OR DO YOU WANT TO DIRECT?"

AFTER GRADUATING FROM HIGH SCHOOL, SPIELBERG hoped to study filmmaking in college. The top college film programs would not accept him, however, because his high school grades were too low. Instead, in 1967 Spielberg enrolled as an English major at California State University at Long Beach, near Los Angeles.

Spielberg was embarrassed by his low high school grades, which were partly due to his poor reading ability. As a child, Spielberg read comic books rather than literature, and he spent more time watching movies and television than he did reading. He later wished he had made himself a stronger reader.

During the summer before college, Spielberg took a tour of Universal Studios in Los Angeles. He wandered away from the tour and struck up conversations with the men and women who made movies at Universal. The next day Spielberg returned to the studio, wearing a suit and carrying a briefcase. He realized that if he simply walked into the studio looking like an important person, the guards at the front gate would not stop him.

Every day that summer, Spielberg, dressed in a suit and tie, explored the Universal lot and talked with directors,

Universal Studios in Los Angeles

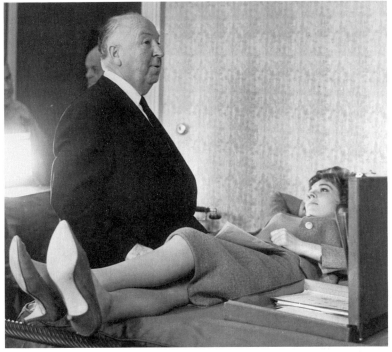

Alfred Hitchcock directs Julie Andrews on the set of Torn Curtain.

writers, and editors. Eventually he found an office that wasn't being used and moved in. He bought plastic letters and put his name in the building directory: "Steven Spielberg, Room 22C."

Spielberg frequently sneaked onto sets where movies were being made. One day he got to see one of his heroes in action. The director Alfred Hitchcock was making a film called *Torn Curtain* at Universal. Spielberg greatly admired the three-hundred-pound, mild-mannered

English director known as "the master of suspense." Hitchcock knew how to build tension in a scene so that audiences were frightened and delighted at the same time. Spielberg relished the chance to see Hitchcock at work. Unfortunately, a Universal security guard discovered Spielberg and threw him off the set.

Spielberg continued to visit the Universal studio even after he began taking college classes. He pestered studio executives into watching his 8-millimeter movies. One of the Universal producers finally told Spielberg that he would have to spend more money on his films and use a 35-millimeter camera if he really wanted to impress anybody. Professional movies are shot on film that is 35 millimeters wide. The wider the film is, the sharper the image and the more vibrant the colors in a movie. Compared to professionally made movies, Spielberg's 8-millimeter films looked small, blurry, and dull when they were projected onto a screen—or a Universal executive's office wall.

Spielberg had a friend named Denis Hoffman who wanted to produce movies. (A producer takes care of the business end of making a movie, while the director is in charge of the artistic aspects.) In 1968 Hoffman agreed to give Spielberg $15,000 to make a 22-minute, 35-millimeter film. The film, called *Amblin',* was about a young couple hitchhiking from the desert to the Pacific Ocean. To keep the film simple, Spielberg told the story without dialogue. He filmed *Amblin'* in ten days and added music and sound effects after the film was shot.

Spielberg now calls *Amblin'* a "slick" film and compares it to "a Pepsi commercial," but the short film served its purpose. It showed people that Steven Spielberg could make a high-quality, professional-looking movie. The executives at Universal Studios were impressed.

The day after *Amblin'* was shown at Universal, Spielberg was called into the office of Sidney Sheinberg, Universal's head of television production. "Sir, I like your work," Sheinberg said. "How would you like to go to work professionally?"

"But I have a year left to go in college," Spielberg said.

"Kid," Sheinberg said, "do you want to go to college or do you want to direct?"

Spielberg and his mentor, Sid Sheinberg

Spielberg had wanted to become a movie director since he was thirteen years old. He could not let the opportunity slip by. He signed a seven-year contract to direct television shows and movies for Universal. "I quit college so fast, I didn't even clean out my locker," Spielberg said.

Sidney Sheinberg became Spielberg's mentor. He provided the young filmmaker with guidance and advice, and over time he gave Spielberg the opportunity to direct more important motion pictures. When Spielberg received a Lifetime Achievement Award from the American Film Institute in 1995, Sidney Sheinberg presented it to him.

Universal purchased the rights to show *Amblin'* in movie theaters. The short film was paired with *Love Story,* one of the most popular feature films of 1970. Years later, when Spielberg started his own production company, he named it Amblin Entertainment, after the movie that launched his professional career.

Spielberg's first assignment at Universal was to direct an episode for a weekly television series called *Night Gallery.* Spielberg directed a story called "Eyes." It was written by Rod Serling, the man who had created both *Night Gallery* and another popular television series, *The Twilight Zone.*

"Eyes" starred old-time screen legend Joan Crawford. Spielberg, five-foot-six and boyish looking at twenty-two, was afraid that a famous star like Crawford would not listen to his directions. Instead, Crawford treated Spielberg with respect. She asked for his advice on how to play her role, and she followed his directions. Just to keep on

Joan Crawford starred in the first episode of Night Gallery *that Spielberg directed.*

the star's good side, Spielberg brought Crawford a rose every day.

In "Eyes," Crawford plays a wealthy New Yorker who has gone blind. She desperately wants to see again, even if only for a short time. She meets a man who has been told by doctors that his eyes will function for just a few more hours. The woman gives the man a fortune in exchange for his eyes. Surgeons transplant his eyes into the woman. Just as her bandages are removed, the whole world goes dark. New York City has gone into a power failure—the famous "blackout" of 1965. The woman's new eyes will fail before the lights come back on.

"Eyes" aired on television on November 8, 1969. Spielberg went on to direct other episodes of *Night Gallery,* as well as episodes of *Marcus Welby, M.D., The Name of the Game, The Psychiatrists,* and *Columbo.* As a television director, Spielberg learned how to work quickly and how to meet a budget. "TV taught me to think on my feet," he said.

Spielberg also learned to tell stories economically. In a television episode, there's not a lot of time to explain things to an audience. Spielberg learned how to get right to the point of a scene. He cut quickly from shot to shot and from scene to scene to hold the audience's attention. Working on television shows, Spielberg became an efficient filmmaker and a clever storyteller.

Spielberg also discovered that it is not always necessary to use big stars. Celebrities can be distracting in a TV show or movie; they call too much attention to themselves. Even after Spielberg became famous, he liked to use good actors who were not very well known. He cast the young Richard Dreyfuss as the hero in *Jaws* and *Close Encounters of the Third Kind* because he thought Dreyfuss had a special talent for playing the underdog, the little guy who triumphs against overwhelming odds.

Working in television, Spielberg developed his skills, but he had little freedom to experiment. He wanted to put his camera in unusual positions or move it in complicated ways, but he soon learned that television shows were filmed in a much more straightforward manner, according to a formula set down by the studios. For

Spielberg, television directing was not an art form; it was just a job.

After two years, Spielberg grew tired of directing television shows. He wanted to make "features," motion pictures that are big enough, long enough (usually an hour and a half to two hours), and important enough to be shown in movie theaters. Under his Universal contract, however, he had to accept the assignments that were given him. His breakthrough came with *Duel,* a 1971 movie made for television. With *Duel,* Spielberg rediscovered the fun of filmmaking.

In tribute to his hero, Alfred Hitchcock, Spielberg's first feature-length film was filled with suspense. *Duel* is a simple story about a salesman named David Mann who is driving through central California on a business trip. On the highway, Mann pulls up behind a huge truck that won't let him pass. When he finally manages to zip past the "road hog," the truck begins to tailgate him. Then it tries to run him off the road. Mann never gets a good look at the truck driver. It seems like the giant truck itself is trying to kill him. No matter what Mann does, the truck is right behind him, slamming into his car, trying to run him over. Finally, after many narrow escapes, the truck and the car lock together and careen over a cliff in a tremendous crash. Mann survives by jumping free at the last second.

Duel was filmed in sixteen days in the California desert on a budget of $425,000. Spielberg asked an artist to draw the whole story of the film on a long strip of paper. He hung this drawing on the wall in his desert motel room, running it all the way around the room like a mural. This way Spielberg could visualize the whole movie at once and think about what part of it he wanted to film each day. "Storyboarding"—sketching action sequences or entire films on paper—became an important tool for Spielberg. With a storyboard, he could come to the set every day fully prepared, knowing just what scenes he wanted to film.

Duel was so popular on American television that Universal decided to release it in movie theaters in Europe. Since the film's story is told largely through action, not words, audiences in any country could enjoy it. As a result of *Duel,* Spielberg became a well-known director in Europe even before he became famous in the U.S.

With the success of *Duel,* Spielberg got the chance to direct a major motion picture. This film, *The Sugarland Express,* was not popular with audiences, but it was well made. The film involved another kind of car chase. This time a whole string of police cars chase a young woman and her husband across the plains of Texas. The couple stage a jailbreak and kidnap a policeman as they head for the town of Sugarland to get their baby back from a foster family. An old Texas ranger tries to bring the couple in safely, but in the end, the husband is shot and killed by the police.

The Sugarland Express convinced Universal executives that Spielberg could handle important movie projects. Spielberg had taken a large crew to Texas, where he spent sixty days filming. He was able to get a strong, serious performance from his star, Goldie Hawn, who was known mainly as a comic actress. He filmed spectacular car crashes, demolishing fifty cars. He staged scenes with 240 cars and 5,000 extras.

On the basis of *The Sugarland Express,* Universal assigned Spielberg to direct *Jaws,* a scary story about a killer shark. *Jaws* was the most difficult film Spielberg ever tried to make. At times, the studio thought about abandoning the film because it was becoming so expensive. When it was finished, however, *Jaws* was more than just a success. It was a film that changed the entire shape of the movie business.

THE BLOCKBUSTER YEARS

JAWS IS THE STORY OF A NEW ENGLAND SEASIDE community that is terrorized by a giant shark. The town's chief of police teams up with a young scientist and an old shark hunter to search for the beast and kill it. The shark, however, sinks the hunters' boat and eats one of the men. The police chief saves himself by wedging an oxygen tank into the monster's mouth.

As the boat sinks, the chief clings to its mast, a few feet above the water. Out on the ocean, the great shark rushes toward him once more. The chief carefully aims his gun at the tank in the shark's mouth. "Smile, you son of a bitch," he says. He fires and hits the tank. It explodes, blowing the shark to smithereens. By killing the shark, the chief has also conquered his fear of water and the dangers that lurk in the deep.

The killer shark in Jaws

Spielberg filmed *Jaws* on the island of Martha's Vineyard, off the coast of Massachusetts. The complicated production was plagued by problems. Three different mechanical sharks were built for the film, and they were all difficult to operate. They sank, their fake skin peeled off, and their hydraulic control systems exploded. Filming on the sea created more problems. Pleasure boats got in the way. Scenes filmed one day on a glassy sea did not match scenes filmed the next day when the sea was rough. Crew members were injured in mysterious accidents. Actor Richard Dreyfuss was heard to mutter, "If any of us had any sense, we'd all bail out now."

Dreyfuss was joking. He trusted Spielberg to get the film made, no matter how long it took. The production schedule allowed fifty-two days for location shooting on Martha's Vineyard. The actual filming took three times that long. Cast and crew members left the island occasionally to take a break from the rigorous filming. Throughout the production, however, Spielberg refused to leave Martha's Vineyard. He said he was afraid that if he left, he would never come back. "*Jaws* was my Vietnam," he said. "It was basically naive people against nature, and nature beat us every day."

As the cost of the film doubled and then tripled, executives at Universal Studios asked producers David Brown and Richard Zanuck to either replace Spielberg or cancel the whole project. The producers refused, and Universal's new president, Sidney Sheinberg, backed them up. Sheinberg had looked at the film's "rushes," the scenes

Spielberg had already completed. Sheinberg saw that his protégé was making a terrific movie.

Jaws was finally completed and released to movie theaters in June 1975. It became the first Hollywood movie to take in more than one hundred million dollars at the box office, breaking the record of eighty-six million dollars set by *The Godfather* in 1972. Richard Zanuck said that he made more money from *Jaws* than his father, Darryl Zanuck, made during his entire thirty-year career running a movie studio.

Because *Jaws* earned so much money, it changed the way many producers thought about filmmaking. Instead of putting up the money for several small, well-made films, producers now hoped to make one hugely successful blockbuster. A single hit like *Jaws* could mean wealth and power for the people who made it. Film studios began to spend more and more money on movies, hoping to hit the jackpot with a blockbuster. By the late 1970s, the fate of an entire studio could depend on the success or failure of a single movie.

Most movies that become blockbusters have certain ingredients. The story must be clear and the characters fairly simple, so the movie is easy for younger viewers and foreign audiences to follow. These are the viewers who will pay to see an exciting movie like *Jaws* or *Star Wars* two or three times.

Studios hope that audiences will want to see a blockbuster again and again. The movie is designed to give viewers plenty of thrills, but not to make them think too

Actor Roy Scheider, producer Richard Zanuck, and director Spielberg take a break on the set of Jaws.

hard. Most blockbusters move at a fast pace, with exciting action and lots of special effects. A blockbuster movie is designed like a roller-coaster ride. (In fact, many blockbuster movies have become roller-coaster rides. Disney and Universal Studios own theme parks that feature thrilling rides based on the films *Star Wars, Back to the Future, Jurassic Park,* and *Indiana Jones and the Temple of Doom.*)

Jaws set the pattern for blockbuster movies. Although the film did not have big stars, it had a well-told story, exciting action, pulsating music, and eye-popping special effects. Universal Studios gave *Jaws* a powerful advertising campaign. The movie's poster became a landmark in American popular culture. It shows the tiny figure of a woman swimming in the ocean. In the water below her looms a killer shark, as big as a house. *Jaws* was also one of the first movies that was widely promoted on television.

Some critics blamed Spielberg for bringing about a new era in Hollywood. Spielberg had made movies more exciting, the critics admitted, but he also made them less serious and less intelligent. This was ironic, because as a young man Spielberg had wanted to make thoughtful "films" instead of merely entertaining "movies." Spielberg probably could not help himself. He liked the same kind of simple but thrilling movies that mass audiences like, and he made those movies more skillfully than anybody else. He became successful as a filmmaker because he shares the tastes of the viewers who pay to see his films.

During the 1960s, Hollywood had lost touch with its audience. In particular, the studios did not seem to know what younger viewers wanted to see. Films like *The Graduate* (1967) and *Easy Rider* (1969) became smash hits because they showed young people rebelling against society's mainstream values. The studios, however, felt safer producing expensive, old-fashioned musicals like *Star!* (1968) and *Darling Lili* (1970), both of which were costly flops.

During the 1970s, the studios turned to young film-makers like Spielberg for new ideas. A group of new young directors in Hollywood became known as the "movie brats." They included Steven Spielberg, George Lucas, Francis Ford Coppola, Martin Scorsese, Brian De Palma, and John Milius, all of whom were born between 1939 and 1947.

In the past, Hollywood directors had learned their craft by working their way up through the ranks of the studio system. (Hollywood studios are somewhat like factories, with workers performing many different jobs along the movie "assembly line.") Many old-time directors began as writers, editors, or assistant directors. By contrast, most of the "movie brats" learned their filmmaking skills in universities. Almost all of them directed feature films while still in their twenties. Together they reshaped the look of Hollywood films in the 1970s with films like *The Godfather* and *Apocalypse Now* (Coppola), *Taxi Driver* (Scorsese), *Carrie* (De Palma), and *American Graffiti* and *Star Wars* (Lucas).

Four of the "movie brats": Francis Ford Coppola (top left), *Martin Scorsese* (top right), *John Milius* (bottom left), *and Brian De Palma* (bottom right).

According to Spielberg, these young filmmakers talked with each other every day. They discussed their movie projects and traded ideas "like kids exchanging baseball cards." For instance, when Spielberg needed to strengthen the shark-hunting sequence in *Jaws,* he called on writer-director John Milius. Milius quickly wrote one of the most powerful speeches in the movie, in which the oldest shark hunter, Quint, describes

> IT WAS A GOLDEN AGE OF FILM-MAKING BECAUSE WE WERE ALL SINGLE, AMBITIOUS, AND IN LOVE WITH FILM.

how the sailors of the USS *Indianapolis,* a ship sunk during World War II, were devoured by sharks. Legend has it that Spielberg and Lucas mapped out plans for *Raiders of the Lost Ark* as they built a sand castle on a beach in Hawaii. Spielberg said, "It was a golden age of filmmaking because we were all single, ambitious, and in love with film."

More than any other filmmakers of the time, Spielberg and Lucas helped reshape Hollywood. Spielberg first met George Lucas at a screening of *THX 1138: 4EB,* a short science fiction film that Lucas made while attending film school at the University of Southern California. Spielberg recognized in Lucas a "kindred spirit," someone who shared his passion and talent for filmmaking. "He reminded me a little bit of Walt Disney's version of a mad scientist," Spielberg said. Over the years, Lucas and Spielberg became filmmaking partners and close friends.

George Lucas made his first hit film in 1973. *American Graffiti* used young actors (including Richard Dreyfuss) and rock and roll music to appeal to youthful audiences. Before *American Graffiti,* Hollywood movies had rarely used rock and roll songs in their sound tracks, since studios had to pay expensive royalty fees for each song they used. Lucas told executives at Universal that he wanted to use eighty popular songs. The executives only wanted to pay for five or six songs at most. Lucas ended up using

Moviemaking pals George Lucas and Steven Spielberg

forty-five songs, creating a pattern for sound tracks that movies have followed ever since.

Lucas was able to make *American Graffiti* the way he wanted to because he had the support of Francis Coppola, a director who had achieved success and power with his own blockbuster film, *The Godfather* (1972). Coppola agreed to act as producer on *American Graffiti.* After *American Graffiti's* first sneak preview in San Francisco, Coppola heard Universal executive Ned Tanen say that he hated the movie and that it was "unreleasable." Standing in the back of the Northpoint Theater, Coppola began to scream at Tanen. "You should go down on your knees and thank George for saving your job," he yelled. Coppola even offered to buy the film from Universal on the spot, but Tanen wisely declined.

Coppola's tirade on behalf of George Lucas and *American Graffiti* became a Hollywood legend. "I wish I'd been there to see it myself," Spielberg once said, "because it's the best story to come out of Hollywood since the late 1940s."

American Graffiti became a hit, and Lucas went on to make the *Star Wars* trilogy, three fantasy films that young audiences loved. While Lucas was directing the first *Star Wars* saga, Spielberg was making his own science fiction film, *Close Encounters of the Third Kind* (1977).

In *Close Encounters,* a group of ordinary people from all around the country are drawn irresistibly to one spot near Devils Tower in Wyoming. Although their friends and families think they have gone crazy, the people find a wonderful surprise at the end of their journey: a huge, pulsating spaceship filled with gentle beings from outer space. For one scene in the movie, Spielberg used his childhood memory of seeing a meteor shower with his father to create a scene with beautiful streaking lights in the sky.

Many people in Hollywood resented Spielberg for becoming so successful before he was thirty years old. "All it took was *Jaws* to be this big hit in 1975," Spielberg said, "and then there were some people who went after *Close Encounters of the Third Kind* as if I had murdered their entire family." It was only in 1982 that Hollywood began to "forgive" Spielberg for his success. That year he released his most popular film, *E.T. The Extra-Terrestrial.* *E.T.* became one of the best-loved movies of all time.

Opposite: *The spaceship from* Close Encounters of the Third Kind

"E.T.
Phone Home"

AFTER THE BLOCKBUSTER SUCCESS OF *JAWS* AND *Close Encounters,* Spielberg experienced his first major failure. He tried to make another blockbuster and it bombed. In 1979 Spielberg directed a World War II comedy called *1941.* The film was based on a real incident in which a Japanese submarine fired shells at an oil refinery along the coast of California.

Spielberg's film emphasized the comic elements of the event: confused Japanese sailors, wacky U.S. pilots, and mixed-up civil defense patrols. The film included a large cast, complicated crowd scenes, and expensive special effects. Its budget soared to forty million dollars. The slapstick humor that Spielberg hoped to achieve, however, got lost in the process of making such a huge film. *Newsweek* critic David Ansen wrote, "Somewhere inside this bloated epic a slim movie is screaming to be heard." Audiences felt worn out by the film rather than amused or entertained.

After *1941* flopped at the box office, Spielberg needed a hit to jump-start his career. He found that hit in *Raiders of the Lost Ark* (1981), an adventure movie directed by Spielberg and produced by George Lucas. *Raiders* was the first of three films that featured the character Indiana Jones. "Indy," played by actor Harrison Ford, is a mild-mannered college professor who leads a double life as a two-fisted, whip-snapping archeologist. In *Raiders of the Lost Ark,* he fights Nazis to gain control over the Biblical Ark of the Covenant. In other adventures, Indy travels to India to recover stones sacred to the Hindu religion (*Indiana Jones and the Temple of Doom,* 1984), and battles the Nazis again in a search for the Holy Grail (*Indiana Jones and the Last Crusade,* 1989).

Indiana Jones became one of the most popular movie heroes of the 1980s. Audiences took comfort in an old-fashioned hero like Indiana Jones. They felt good cheering for an "ordinary guy" who uses his fists and his wits to survive. Throughout the 1980s, Spielberg used the adventures of Indiana Jones to maintain his position as Hollywood's most popular filmmaker.

While he was filming *Raiders of the Lost Ark,* Spielberg worked out the idea for *E.T.* At first Spielberg thought he wanted to make a movie about aliens invading Earth, a scary sequel to *Close Encounters of the Third Kind.* He wrote a story called "Night Skies" and asked writer-director John Sayles to develop it as an outline for a screenplay. When Spielberg saw Sayles's treatment of the story, he realized that he liked one small, friendly alien more than the other hostile invaders. He began to focus on the friendly alien. "What if he got left behind?" Spielberg wondered. "What if the little chap, the straggler, missed the bus home?"

Spielberg was shooting *Raiders* on location in Tunisia when screenwriter Melissa Mathison arrived to visit actor Harrison Ford. (Mathison and Ford were later married.) Mathison had cowritten the screenplay for *The Black Stallion* (1979), a polished and popular children's movie produced by Francis Coppola. Since then she had

Melissa Mathison and her husband, Harrison Ford

grown frustrated with screenwriting, and she had turned down an earlier offer to work on *E.T.* Spielberg, however, got Mathison interested in his new ideas about the story of a stranded alien. Together they began to work out the details of E.T.'s adventure, and Mathison returned to the United States to write the screenplay.

To design the lovable extraterrestrial for *E.T.,* Spielberg hired Carlo Rambaldi, a sculptor who had created a giant

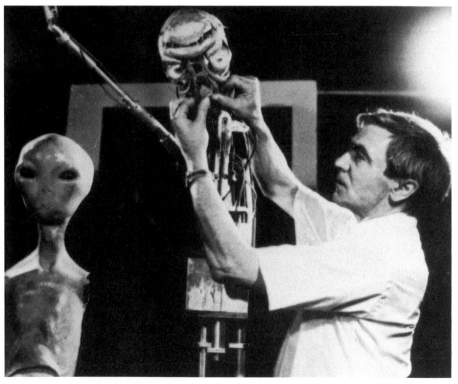

Carlo Rambaldi designed E.T.

ape for *King Kong* (1976) and a big-headed, gruesome monster for *Alien* (1979). Rambaldi and his coworkers spent more than 5,000 hours creating three separate versions of E.T. They built a mechanical model that could walk by itself, an electronic model whose facial muscles could be operated by remote control, and an E.T. "suit" that was worn by several small actors, including a boy who had been born without legs. E.T.'s voice was provided by Pat Welsh, a woman in her sixties, with added vocal effects by the actress Debra Winger. Filming began in September 1981, and the movie was finished and released to theaters the following June.

E.T. is the story of a ten-year-old boy named Elliott who finds a creature from outer space in his backyard. Elliott does not have many friends. His older brother has little time for him. His younger sister is a pest. His mother always seems frantic, trying to work at a job and raise three kids at the same time.

Significantly, Elliott's father does not live with the family. As in many Spielberg films, the missing father is an important theme in *E.T.* Like many Spielberg heroes, Elliott wants to find a "father figure," a strong man who can take care of those weaker than himself. Elliott even tries to become a father figure to the extraterrestrial, or "E.T.," who has been left behind by his spaceship.

At first Elliott treats E.T. like a child. He teaches the little creature about candy and television and comic books. He rescues E.T. from danger. Then, as the film progresses, Elliott and E.T. learn to be brave together. They share comic adventures. They go trick-or-treating together and they accidentally get drunk on beer.

Finally, E.T. becomes a kind of father to Elliott. The little space being is really old and wise. He teaches Elliott that the bravest thing anyone can do is to love somebody else. Early in the film, E.T. learns to say "ouch" when he hurts his finger. At the end of the film, when E.T.'s spaceship returns for him, he says "ouch" again. This time he says it to express the pain he feels in his heart. Elliott and E.T. have learned to feel the same things, and the strongest feeling is love.

Director of photography Allen Daviau

Critics and audiences praised *E.T.* for its style as well as its story. Spielberg placed lights behind characters so that they seemed to glow with power and mystery. This "back-lighting" was a technique that Spielberg had worked on for years. With *E.T.,* it became a trademark of his style.

E.T.'s director of photography, who handled the film's lighting and the placement, movement, and focusing of the camera, was Allen Daviau. Years before, Daviau had worked for low pay as the cameraman on *Amblin'.* Spielberg had promised Daviau that someday they would make feature films together. In 1981, Daviau was filming television commercials when Spielberg, repaying the old debt, asked him to film *E.T.* After *E.T.,* Daviau became one of the most sought-after cinematographers in Hollywood. He worked again with Spielberg as director of photography on *The Color Purple* and *Empire of the Sun.*

Many critics have noted that Spielberg's films often have a "longing for home" theme. The space alien E.T. yearns to return to his home planet. In *Jaws,* as the shark hunters await their final battle with the monster, a song— "Show Me the Way to Go Home"—brings them closer together. The lost children in *Hook* (1991) and the stolen children in *Indiana Jones and the Temple of Doom* ache to rejoin their families. Spielberg has said that the "longing for home" theme in his movies comes from his own childhood memories.

E.T. was so popular with audiences that an image and a line of dialogue from the film entered American popular culture. The line occurs when E.T. decides to build a

With E.T., *Spielberg created a pop culture phenomenon.*

transmitter to contact his own planet. "E.T. phone home," the alien tells Elliott. That line became a popular saying in the 1980s, just as "May the Force be with you" (from *Star Wars*) and "Make him an offer he can't refuse" (from *The Godfather*) were popular sayings in the 1970s.

The most famous image from *E.T.* comes at the end of the film. Elliott and the neighborhood boys are racing on their bicycles to return E.T. to his spaceship. They are being chased by police cars and government vans. The boys cut across parks and vacant lots, but finally they are trapped by a roadblock. At that point, E.T. uses his superhuman powers to send the bicycles flying through the air. Elliott, who is carrying E.T. in a basket on the front of his bicycle, soars into the sky. That image—the silhouette of a boy flying across the outline of the moon—was deeply moving to viewers. Spielberg gave people a beautiful reminder of what it means to think and feel and dream with the heart of a child.

Spielberg and his first wife, Amy Irving, had a son, Max, in 1985.

"It's Not the Years That Kill You, It's the Mileage"

RAIDERS OF THE LOST ARK, E.T., AND *INDIANA Jones and the Temple of Doom* gave Spielberg three smash hits in a row. Despite his popularity, Spielberg suffered many setbacks in the 1980s. The character Indiana Jones once said, "It's not the years that kill you, it's the mileage." During the 1980s, Spielberg traveled down some bumpy roads. The journey did not kill him, but it made him wiser.

In 1982 Spielberg coproduced and codirected a movie based on the old television series *The Twilight Zone.* Spielberg's contribution to *Twilight Zone—The Movie* was an episode called "Kick the Can." In "Kick the Can," a group of bored, unhappy senior citizens begin to play a simple children's game. Magically, they become children again. Spielberg spent just six days filming this story. He made the short film quickly because he wanted to get away from the whole *Twilight Zone* project. Disaster had struck one of *Twilight Zone*'s other episodes.

Spielberg's coproducer, John Landis, was directing the biggest and most expensive of *Twilight Zone*'s four stories. In the Landis segment, actor Vic Morrow plays a bigot, a man who hates people who are different from him. Leaving a bar one night, the bigot steps into the "Twilight Zone." He finds himself tumbling through time, popping up in one place and then another. In each place he suffers persecution at the hands of other bigots. He is a Jew in Nazi Germany, an African American who is nearly lynched by the Ku Klux Klan, and a Vietnamese soldier who must save a pair of children from a frightening helicopter attack.

During the filming of the helicopter attack, Landis insisted on realism. Violating child labor laws, he brought two young children to a rugged location late at night. He insisted that the helicopter fly low, through gigantic special-effects explosions, just twenty-four feet above Vic Morrow and the children.

The result was disastrous. The violent explosions sent the helicopter spinning out of control. Its blades slicing the air, the helicopter crashed. It landed on Vic Morrow and the children, killing all three of them.

John Landis was brought to trial for his reckless actions. A jury acquitted him of charges of involuntary manslaughter. Landis was not punished, but he admitted that he had broken labor laws.

Above: *Crews clean up the wreckage of the helicopter that crashed on the set of* The Twilight Zone, *killing actor Vic Morrow and two children.* Left: *Director John Landis testifies at the manslaughter trial that resulted from the crash.*

Steven Spielberg was not responsible for the tragedy of *Twilight Zone—The Movie.* He was, however, the co-producer of the film. In their book *Outrageous Conduct,* authors Stephen Farber and Marc Green argue that it was Spielberg's job to know what was going on. He should have known that children were hired illegally in the making of the film. If that is true, Spielberg failed in his job. He never acknowledged that failure. Over the years, he has tried to distance himself from the movie.

The next controversy in Spielberg's career involved *Indiana Jones and the Temple of Doom.* Audiences were shocked by the film's violence. Critics had complained earlier that *Poltergeist,* a film Spielberg wrote and pro-duced in 1982, was too violent for young children. *Temple of Doom* included even more violent scenes, such as a man getting his heart ripped out of his chest. Both *Polter-geist* and *Temple of Doom* were very popular with audi-ences, but protests led Hollywood studios to create a new rating, "PG-13," for movies that were considered too vio-lent for children under age thirteen.

During the 1980s, Spielberg's personal life was as rocky as his career. He had begun dating the actress Amy Irving in the mid-1970s. The daughter of an actress mother and a theater director father, Irving was seven years younger than Spielberg. She made her film debut in the horror movie *Carrie* (1976) and was nominated for an Academy Award for Best Supporting Actress for her role in Barbra Streisand's film *Yentl* (1983). At one point Spielberg and Irving flew to Japan, planning to be married. Before the

Amy Irving and Spielberg began dating in the 1970s.

marriage could take place, however, the couple broke up. Spielberg would not tell his friends what had gone wrong.

In 1980 Spielberg began dating Kathleen Carey, a junior executive in the music industry. Spielberg hoped that he might be able to start a family with Carey, but she broke off the relationship. "I cried for the first time in ages," Spielberg said.

Spielberg then reconciled with Amy Irving. The couple gave birth to a son, Max, in June 1985. Spielberg said that making *E.T.* made him realize he wanted to have children. Making *E.T.,* he told interviewer Denise Worrell, was like "tasting what it would be like to be a daddy and really opening my heart up for the first time to the possibilities of being a father to my own kids."

Amy Irving and Steven Spielberg were married in November 1985. The marriage was happy at first. The couple moved into a fourteen-room mansion in Beverly Hills and spent weekends at Spielberg's beach house in Malibu. They did not attend many big Hollywood parties. Instead, they spent their evenings watching films, playing video games, and eating pizza and junk food.

Before long, however, the marriage began to collapse. Personal problems and pressures from their separate careers drove the couple apart. Biographer Douglas Brode thinks it may have been Spielberg's obsession with movies that drove a wedge between him and his wife. "The only time I feel totally happy is when I'm watching films or making them," Spielberg said. The place where Spielberg was most happy was not at home, but at his

Irving and Spielberg divorced in 1989.

rambling, Spanish-style office on the lot at Universal Studios. For Spielberg, filmmaking was still a golden shield against fear and failure—including the failure of his marriage.

Divorce had been the word Spielberg dreaded most as a child. Now he found himself saying it. Spielberg and Irving suffered through a bitter divorce in 1989. Throughout his personal ups and   lberg devoted

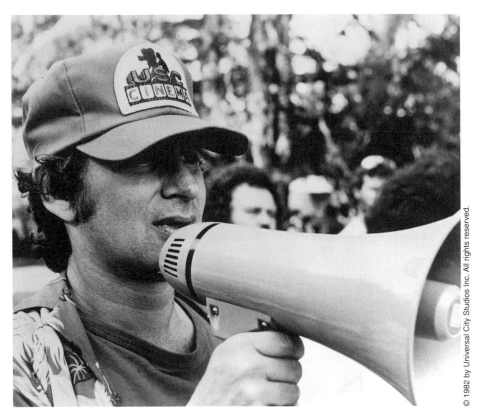

Spielberg demands top performances from himself and from everyone who works for him.

himself to filmmaking. He said that he often did his best work when he felt the worst about his personal life.

Spielberg was not always easy to work for. He insisted on perfection, from himself and others. Employees who did not deliver top performances were quickly let go. Spielberg could be cold, and he often kept himself apart from his workers. His mother once joked that when people stopped working for Spielberg, they ceased to exist as far as he was concerned.

At the same time, Spielberg was loyal to his friends and generous in giving credit to his coworkers. He has said that he owes much of the success of his films to two key people, editor Michael Kahn and music composer John Williams. Kahn has edited eleven of Spielberg's fifteen feature films. Williams composed the music for thirteen of those films (as well as the score to George Lucas's *Star Wars* series).

> THROUGHOUT HIS PERSONAL UPS AND DOWNS, SPIELBERG DEVOTED HIMSELF TO FILMMAKING. HE SAID THAT HE OFTEN DID HIS BEST WORK WHEN HE FELT THE WORST ABOUT HIS PERSONAL LIFE.

During the 1980s, Spielberg was growing as a man and as an artist. On a list of the best Hollywood movies of all time, many people would include *Jaws, E.T.,* and *Raiders of the Lost Ark.* None of Spielberg's films, however, dealt with complex, serious, "adult" relationships. According to author Douglas Brode, "Critics loudly demanded to know if the boy genius would ever become a mature filmmaker or forever remain Peter Pan with a movie camera."

In 1986, Spielberg received the Irving Thalberg Memorial Award from the Academy of Motion Picture Arts and Sciences for his special contributions to the film industry.

GETTING
SERIOUS

WOULD SPIELBERG EVER BE A "SERIOUS" DIRECTOR? As if to answer his critics, Spielberg directed three serious films: *The Color Purple* (1985), *Empire of the Sun* (1987), and *Always* (1989). All of these films were well made, but none of them was completely successful.

The Color Purple is set in rural Georgia during the period from 1909 to 1937. It is the story of Celie, an African American woman who, as a girl, is raped by a man she believes to be her father. Her two babies are taken away from her, and all her life she wonders if she will ever see her children again. She is forced to marry a cruel older man, whom she calls "Mister." Mister separates Celie from her beloved sister Nettie, and over the years he hides the letters that Nettie writes to Celie.

What helps Celie survive and grow strong is her friendship with other women. Sophia, a large, powerful woman, shows Celie how to stand up to her husband. Sophia

fights her own husband, slugs another woman, and hits a
white man who slaps her and treats her with disrespect.
For that last act, a serious offense in the racist South of the
time, Sophia is harshly punished. She is pistol-whipped,
then thrown into prison for eight years. The "white folks"
almost break Sophia's spirit, but her strength and courage
return when she sees Celie finally stand up to Mister and
call him "a lowdown dirty dog."

The other woman who helps Celie is Shug Avery,
Mister's girlfriend. Shug is a beautiful, fashionable woman
who works as a blues singer in nightclubs. She teaches
Celie to love life. "More than anything, God loves admi-
ration," Shug tells Celie. "I think it pisses God off if you
walk by the color purple in a field and don't notice it."

In the end, Celie finds the strength to leave Mister.
Mister tells Celie that she will never survive without
him. She is just a poor, black, ugly woman, he says. As
she drives away, Celie yells back at Mister. "I'm poor,
black, I may even be ugly," she says. "But, dear God, I'm
here. I'm here!"

Celie is reunited with her two grown children, who
have been living with Nettie in Africa. Her son and
daughter have been raised with the strength and pride of
their African ancestors. In the last scene of the film, Celie
and Nettie sit together at sunset in a field of purple flow-
ers, playing a hand-clapping game that they played as little girls.

The making of *The Color Purple* was surrounded by
controversy. The film was based on the Pulitzer Prize-

winning novel by Alice Walker. Many African Americans were troubled by Walker's novel. They felt that it portrayed African American men as monsters. People protesting the film picketed outside the office of the film's producer, Quincy Jones.

Other people supported the book's message. They felt that women, especially black women, had suffered for too many years. Alice Walker was speaking up for women.

Alice Walker, author of The Color Purple

Readers who responded to Walker's message, however, thought Spielberg was the wrong person to turn the novel into a film. They worried that because Spielberg usually made "fun" movies, he would soften the powerful impact of the book. A joke circulated in Hollywood that the film would be called "Steven Spielberg's *Close Encounters of the Third World.*" Even Spielberg wondered if he was the right director for the film. "Don't you want to find a black director or a woman?" he asked Quincy Jones.

Jones wanted Spielberg to direct the film for two reasons. First, he needed Spielberg's clout. With Spielberg's name on *The Color Purple,* the movie would definitely get made, and it would be seen. The Spielberg name alone would draw millions of viewers to the box office. Secondly, Jones knew that Spielberg believed in the project. Spielberg loved Walker's novel and had many ideas about how to turn it into a movie. When Alice Walker met Spielberg, she agreed that he was the right director for *The Color Purple.*

In the end, though, no one was entirely happy with Spielberg's version of *The Color Purple.* The film was beautifully photographed by Allen Daviau, but it seemed almost too beautiful. Daviau and Spielberg created a gentle, romantic view of rural Georgia. (The film was actually shot in North Carolina. Two planeloads of red clay from Georgia were flown to the location.) Critics complained that *The Color Purple* did not realistically depict the difficult life of African Americans. In Spielberg's movie, no one was poor or hungry or forced to work hard.

Spielberg directs Whoopi Goldberg in The Color Purple.

The world Alice Walker created in her novel was much harsher. *New York Times* film critic Janet Maslin complained that the movie lacked "realism and grit."

Spielberg did direct some of the strongest adult performances of his career in *The Color Purple.* Actor Danny Glover made Mister a complex, frightening character. The comedian Whoopi Goldberg became an instant movie star through her portrayal of Celie. Talk-show host Oprah Winfrey played proud, fiery Sophia. Spielberg faced his biggest challenge in presenting the crucial relationship between Celie and Shug Avery (played by Margaret Avery). In Alice Walker's book, Shug and Celie have a love affair. In the film, Spielberg uses hesitant, tender kisses to hint at the love between the two women. Some critics accused him of backing away from the more adult themes of Walker's book. Spielberg defended himself by saying that he was more interested in the love between the women than the sex.

The novel *The Color Purple* challenges the reader's values. Spielberg's movie is powerful and even shocking in places, but it does not challenge the values of the audience. The film does what Spielberg movies always do—it praises the human spirit. It shows a mother struggling to hold on to her children, just like Goldie Hawn's character Lou Jean in *The Sugarland Express* and Jilian, the mother whose little boy is snatched away by aliens in *Close Encounters of the Third Kind.* Under Spielberg's direction, *The Color Purple* became another tribute to ordinary people who have the courage to face danger and the strength to triumph over hardship.

Spielberg's next film was one of his least popular. *Empire of the Sun* was the first Hollywood film to include scenes shot in the People's Republic of China. Spielberg went on location to Shanghai, China, where he restaged the Japanese invasion of that city during World War II. Spielberg filmed huge crowd scenes for the invasion, using thousands of Chinese extras.

In the midst of the swirling crowds, a British boy, Jim Graham, becomes separated from his parents. Jim is forced to spend the war in a Japanese prison camp. He suffers from hunger and exhaustion, but he learns to survive. Needing a father figure, Jim turns to Basie, a thieving scoundrel who betrays Jim and abandons him. In the end, Jim is restored to his parents, but he is not the same happy child he once was.

With *Empire of the Sun,* Spielberg again tried to make a serious film. But audiences found the movie gloomy and confusing. The film was based on a novel by J. G. Ballard, which was turned into a screenplay by British playwright Tom Stoppard. Both Stoppard and Ballard had a more cynical view of Jim than Spielberg did. Spielberg could not help seeing the innocence in the boy. As a result, the film seems to contradict itself. It is neither as sad as the writers intended, nor as hopeful as Spielberg might have wanted it. One critic called the film "a curious case of arrested development." Spielberg would not let either Jim or his film grow up.

The character Jim in *Empire of the Sun* is in love with planes. He clutches a small model plane in his hand as his parents pull him through the crowded streets of Shanghai. When he drops the plane and stoops to retrieve it, he lets go of his mother's hand. By the time he has picked up the plane, his parents have been swept away by the crowd. Later, Jim develops a special bond with a young Japanese fighter pilot, even though the Japanese are supposed to be his enemies.

Many of Spielberg's other films also make use of airplanes and the theme of flying. Spielberg used old fighter planes and a dirigible to create a thrilling action sequence in *Indiana Jones and the Last Crusade. Indiana Jones and the Temple of Doom* and *1941* both include airplane crashes. In *E.T.,* Elliott flies on his bicycle, and in *Hook* (1991), Peter Pan becomes a hero when he remembers how to fly.

Spielberg's fascination with flying probably comes from his father, who served as a radioman on a B-25 bomber plane in World War II. In 1989, Spielberg decided to make a movie about fliers. He patterned his film after an old Hollywood movie called *A Guy Named Joe* (1944). The earlier film was a story about World War II pilots. Spielberg's film, called *Always,* was about modern-day pilots who use their planes to fight forest fires.

Always has tender love scenes and many special effects, but something is missing. When the pilots are up in the air fighting fires, the film is exciting. On the ground, it moves too slowly. One critic thought the film suffered from Spielberg's decision to set the story in modern times. The men and women in *A Guy Named Joe* were wartime heroes, fighting for a cause bigger than themselves. The heroes in *Always* never seem quite so big or so noble.

> BY BEING SO HEAVY-HANDED, SPIELBERG FORGOT ONE OF THE OLDEST RULES OF HOLLYWOOD FILMMAKING: THE STORY COMES FIRST.

Spielberg followed *Always* with *Hook* (1991), a retelling of the story of Peter Pan. *Hook* was lavishly produced, but it was a bit too complicated for children and too childish for adults. Audiences also felt that Spielberg was hitting them over the head with the message that parents should be responsible and loving to their children. By being so heavy-handed, Spielberg forgot one of the oldest rules of Hollywood filmmaking: the story comes first. Samuel Goldwyn, an old-time movie producer, once said, "When I want to send a message, I call Western Union."

Empire of the Sun, Always, and *Hook* were not well received by critics or audiences. Spielberg needed a hit. He had spent seventy-nine million dollars making *Hook.* He thought *Hook* might be his last big film. He was wrong. His next movie cost sixty-five million dollars, but it was worth it. *Jurassic Park* became the biggest money-making movie of its time.

Spielberg with his second wife, Kate Capshaw

"THE *T. REX* OF DIRECTORS"

IN 1991 SPIELBERG MARRIED HIS SECOND WIFE, actress Kate Capshaw, one of the stars of *Indiana Jones and the Temple of Doom.* Capshaw, born in Texas in 1953, was a schoolteacher before she became an actress (she holds a master's degree in special education). She started her acting career in New York, performing in television commercials and soap operas before breaking into the movies in 1982. She shares Spielberg's love of movies, and she enjoys her husband's constant habit of comparing real-life situations to scenes he remembers from old movies.

Before her marriage to Spielberg, Capshaw converted to Judaism. It was something she had been thinking about doing for years, and meeting Spielberg and his family convinced her that the time was right. "It was important to me," she said, "to feel as legitimate on the inside as on the outside."

Capshaw says she gets along well with Spielberg's previous wife, Amy Irving ("so much so that Amy and I agree
it would make a great sitcom"). Capshaw and Spielberg
are raising a "blended" family of their own children, children they have adopted, and children from their previous
marriages. Their six children are named Max, Theo,
Jessica, Sawyer, Sasha, and Mikaela.

Mikaela first saw her father when he appeared on television at the 1996 Academy Awards show. Her mother
held Mikaela in front of the television screen and said,
"Look, honey, there's your daddy." The baby burped.

Spielberg says that his wife and family have helped
him to understand himself. "Now, thanks to Katie and
my . . . amazing kids," Spielberg says, "I know who I am
without the script."

Steven Spielberg has been influenced by many other
filmmakers whose movies he watched as a child and
studied as an adult. Spielberg has said that the one film
that probably influenced him the most was the ballet film
The Red Shoes (1948) by British director Michael Powell.
Another British director, David Lean (*Lawrence of
Arabia, Dr. Zhivago*), provided a model for Spielberg's
work as a director. Lean's pictures, like Spielberg's, com-
bine intimate human dramas and epic events.

Spielberg also has praised the work of the great American director John Ford, who made 130 films during his
long career in Hollywood. (By contrast, Spielberg had
made only eighteen feature films by the age of 50.) Spiel-

WOW

David Lean was one of the directors whom Spielberg admired.

berg admires the "workhorses" of the old Hollywood studio system, directors like Michael Curtiz (*Casablanca*)
and Victor Fleming (*The Wizard of Oz, Gone With the
Wind*), who could turn out two or three films a year.
Most of all, Spielberg has been influenced by the suspense films directed by Alfred Hitchcock (*Psycho, The
Birds*) and the children's films produced by Walt Disney.

Walt Disney did more than make children's films. He
demonstrated that a movie can be the center of a giant
merchandising operation. For Disney, a movie was not

*Walt Disney turned his film characters into an amusement park
empire that includes Disneyland and Walt Disney World.*

simply a story to be told. It was also a wellspring of products: mugs and mouse ears and beach towels and Davy Crockett coonskin caps. A movie was a potential amusement-park ride. It was an opportunity to "spin off" television shows, and it was the source for recorded music albums. For better or worse, Disney changed the nature of the movie business by showing filmmakers how to sell hundreds of products based on their movies.

Disney was ahead of his time; not until the 1970s did other major studios begin to follow his example. George Lucas led the way, turning his *Star Wars* films into a sales bonanza of toys, T-shirts, and even a ride at Disneyland. By the 1980s, almost every blockbuster film was designed with mass-merchandising opportunities in mind. When Steven Spielberg released *Jurassic Park* to movie theaters in June 1993, over one thousand "officially licensed" products were linked to the film. *Jurassic Park* screenwriter David Koepp once laughingly remarked, "Here I was writing about these greedy people who are creating a fabulous theme park just so they can exploit all these dinosaurs and make silly little films and sell stupid plastic plates and things. And I'm writing it for a company that's eventually going to put this in their theme parks and make these silly little films and sell stupid plastic plates. I was really chasing my tail there for a while."

Jurassic Park was in preproduction for two years before actual filming began. Several writers were asked to provide different versions of the screenplay, which was based on a novel by best-selling author Michael Crichton.

Design teams created paintings of the different animals and environments in *Jurassic Park*. Other artists worked with Spielberg to produce storyboards—shot-by-shot drawings—of the seven or eight crucial action scenes in the novel. Most importantly, three different companies were hired to design full-size, miniature, and computer-generated dinosaurs for the film. Ideas were continually being tried out and rejected. "It was like survival of the fittest," said production designer Rick Carter.

The years of preparation paid off when it came time to shoot the film. Spielberg and his crew worked quickly and efficiently, the dinosaurs looked more realistic than anyone had thought possible, and even a hurricane could not throw the film off schedule.

Spielberg chose to shoot the film's location scenes in Hawaii rather than in Costa Rica, where the story was set. (He said he liked the idea of staying in a comfortable Hawaiian hotel with room service and a pool, rather than traveling to some rugged, remote location.) Hawaii provided beautiful scenery, and filming went smoothly until a day before the end of the shoot. Then, on Friday, September 11, 1992, Hurricane Iniki struck the Hawaiian island of Kauai. Spielberg and the 140 members of his cast and crew huddled in their hotel's ballroom for seven and a half hours while winds up to 180 miles an hour raged outside.

When he stepped outside the following morning, Spielberg saw that the hurricane had uprooted trees and telephone poles, blown off roofs, and crumbled walls.

The Velociraptor *model from the* Jurassic Park *exhibit at Universal Studios.*

"Iniki had gone through Kauai like the big bad wolf at the house made of straw," Spielberg said. Fortunately, no one was hurt, and by the following Tuesday, shooting on *Jurassic Park* had resumed at Universal Studios.

Actress Laura Dern, who plays Dr. Ellie Sadler in *Jurassic Park,* said that Hurricane Iniki was "a bonding experience" for the cast and crew. "We became real family," Dern said. When asked if Steven Spielberg was a strict or demanding director, Dern said, "It's not that he's strict but that he's so well prepared. He knows exactly what he wants." Dern had expected Spielberg to act like an "important person," not someone who would spend extra time with the cast and crew. Instead, she said, Spielberg plays and laughs and talks with his cast and crew. "Then he tells us to get back to work," said Dern. "But he never yells."

Much of *Jurassic Park* was shot on soundstages at Universal Studios in Los Angeles. Several of the film's major scenes, including the final battle between a *Tyrannosaurus rex* and two *Velociraptors,* were created on a computer. For those scenes, the performers had to act amazed or terrified even though they actually could not see the dinosaurs, which were added to the film after the humans' performances were shot. Actor Sam Neill, who plays Dr. Alan Grant, said that it was sometimes difficult to act awestruck or afraid of dinosaurs that were not really there.

As the film begins, the Jurassic Park theme park is not yet open to the public, and already things are going wrong. A worker has been killed, pulled inside an animal cage and ripped to pieces. Lawyers are threatening to close the park before it opens. The park's creator, John Hammond, brings in three scientists to examine Jurassic Park and pronounce it safe. The scientists are stunned to learn that Hammond has filled his park with real, living dinosaurs.

As the scientists tour the park, accompanied by Hammond's grandchildren and a lawyer, catastrophe strikes. The animals break loose from their enclosures and terrorize the visitors. A *Tyrannosaurus rex* stomps on the tour cars, crushes mathematician Ian Malcom, and devours the lawyer. Paleontologist Dr. Alan Grant is forced to spend a night up in a tree, with Hammond's grandchildren huddling close to him for protection. The scientist squirms uncomfortably. Children make him nervous.

By contrast, Grant's partner, paleobotanist Dr. Ellie Sadler, likes children. She wants to marry Grant and start a family. While Grant and the children trek across Jurassic Park to safety, Sadler rescues the injured Ian Malcom. Together they flee another attack by the *Tyrannosaurus rex,* which comes crashing down the road after them.

With the dinosaurs roaming out of control, John Hammond and his visitors prepare to leave the park in a helicopter. First, however, the group must escape a pair of deadly *Velociraptors.* The raptors are vicious, six-foot-tall dinosaurs who hunt their prey with keen intelligence and razor-sharp claws. The raptors corner Grant, Sadler, and the children in the park's visitor center. Just as the raptors are closing in for the kill, the *Tyrannosaurus rex* crashes through the wall and lunges at the raptors. During the melee that follows, the humans sneak out the door.

As Hammond's helicopter flies away from the park, the children draw close to Dr. Grant, who puts his arms around them protectively. Ellie Sadler smiles at Grant. It appears that he has changed his mind about children. Outside the window, Grant sees a flock of pelicans flying over the ocean. He smiles wistfully. He knows that birds are the last remaining descendants of the dinosaurs.

Spielberg originally planned to use a combination of full-size and miniature dinosaur models for *Jurassic Park*. A team of workers headed by special-effects wizard Stan Winston created the full-size creatures. They built a 20-foot-tall *Tyrannosaurus rex* that weighed 13,000 pounds. For the *Velociraptors,* Winston's team imal suit that could be worn by an a mechanical puppet. Several people w ate the puppet for a scene in whic Hammond's grandchildren in a large kitchen. "On it it was actually more hilarious than frightening," Spielberg said, "because just under the kids there would be three operators with remote controls, another six operators underneath the camera, twelve operators hiding in the cabinetry. The actors were literally stepping over operators to go through the actions of the scene."

Throughout the filming of *Jurassic Park,* Spielberg emphasized that the dinosaurs were animals, not monsters.

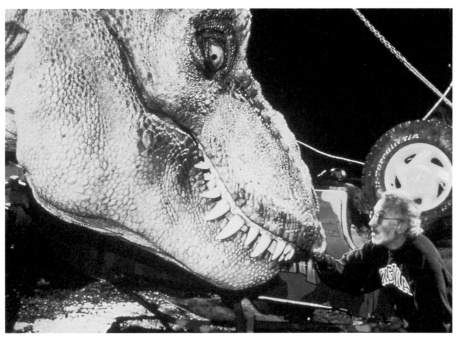

Stan Winston created full-size dinosaur models for Jurassic Park.

They might be scary, but they should be scary in the way that a hungry lion or tiger is scary. Stan Winston and the other special-effects artists spent months studying the muscles, movements, and sounds of living animals, including elephants, giraffes, and whales.

Spielberg planned to use miniature models for about fifty shots in *Jurassic Park*. For one scene, he wanted to show a whole herd of dinosaurs stampeding across a valley. Concerned that such a scene would not look realistic with model puppets, Spielberg turned to the computer graphics team at Industrial Light and Magic, a special-effects company founded by George Lucas. The ILM team not only produced a believable-looking stampede, they also created a computer-generated *Tyrannosaurus rex.* When the *T. rex* appeared onscreen, ILM's Dennis Murren said, "Everybody went absolutely crazy. It was like nothing anyone had seen before." The ILM team had advanced the state of the art of computer graphics. When Spielberg saw the computer-generated *T. rex,* he decided to abandon the miniature models that had been developed for the film. (Model maker Phil Tippett said he felt like he had become extinct.) Except for Stan Winston's

A Sega employee works on a Jurassic Park *video game.*

full-size creatures, all the dinosaur shots in *Jurassic Park* were done on the computer.

Dean Cundey, the director of photography for *Jurassic Park,* said that Spielberg "wanted a very realistic look for Jurassic Park, so that the audience would feel as if they were *in* the park, as much as possible." Cundey and Spielberg succeeded in placing viewers inside a remarkable world that seemed to bring both the past and the future into the present.

Audiences were thrilled, and *Jurassic Park* took in nine hundred million dollars at the box office worldwide. The film surged ahead of *E.T.* as the biggest moneymaker of all time. Once again, Spielberg proved that he was, in the words of his friend George Lucas, "the *T. rex* of directors."

Spielberg and Thomas Keneally, author of the book Schindler's List

CHAPTER EIGHT

"Whoever Saves One Life Saves the World Entire"

In 1980, an Australian writer named Thomas Keneally entered a luggage store in Beverly Hills. Keneally was shopping for a briefcase. What he found was a fascinating story. The owner of the store, Poldek Pfefferberg, was a Jewish man who had lived through the Holocaust of World War II. Pfefferberg told Keneally that his life had been saved by a German businessman named Oskar Schindler. In fact, Schindler saved the lives of hundreds of Jews. Pfefferberg insisted that Keneally should write a book about this remarkable man.

With the help of Pfefferberg and many of the other "Schindler Jews," Keneally was able to piece together the story of Oskar Schindler. He published that story in 1982 as the book *Schindler's List*. Steven Spielberg bought the rights to make a movie based on Keneally's book. It took several years, however, before anyone could figure out how to turn the book into a dramatic screenplay. Finally, screenwriter Steven Zaillian wrote a screenplay that Spielberg felt was right. Universal Studios agreed to pay the cost of making the movie, twenty-three million dollars.

Spielberg considered using Harrison Ford, the star of the *Indiana Jones* films, to play Schindler. In the end, however, he decided he wanted an actor who was not too familiar to moviegoers. He happened to see the Irish actor Liam Neeson appearing on Broadway in the play *Anna Christie*. After the play, Spielberg took his wife, Kate Capshaw, and her mother backstage to meet Neeson. Neeson noticed that Spielberg's mother-in-law was crying. Apparently she had been deeply moved by the play. Without even thinking about it, the tall Irishman took this stranger in his arms and hugged her.

Later Kate Capshaw said to her husband, "That's exactly what Schindler would have done." Spielberg agreed. Liam Neeson, he decided, should play Schindler.

For the crucial supporting role of Itzhak Stern, Schindler's accountant, Spielberg chose Ben Kingsley, who won an Academy Award for his performance in the 1982 film *Gandhi.* Kingsley said that he was almost overwhelmed by the pain and suffering of the Jews who were portrayed in the film. "I was afraid that the boundaries between actor and role would collapse," he said, "that my colossal grief would make me unable to perform."

Spielberg himself was torn between overwhelming emotions and a strong sense of purpose. To broaden his

Liam Neeson starred in Schindler's List.

own knowledge of the Holocaust, he watched the nine-hour documentary *Shoah,* by French filmmaker Claude Lanzmann, four times. In the past, Spielberg had forced himself to visit concentration camps. The experience had left him feeling angry and helpless. Now as he prepared to make *Schindler's List,* he realized he was not helpless in the face of the Holocaust. There was something he could do to make a difference. He could make a movie.

Spielberg felt a powerful sense of responsibility to make *Schindler's List,* for himself, for his Jewish heritage, for the Jews who died in the Holocaust, and for those who survived. If his gift was the ability to tell stories through the medium of film, then his obligation was to tell this story for Jews everywhere. This time he would not hide behind the shield of his movie camera but would risk his own feelings as a Jew and as a man.

To make *Schindler's List,* Spielberg needed all the film-making skills he had acquired during his twenty years as a director. *Schindler's List* has large crowd scenes and small, tender moments. One hundred and twenty-six actors have speaking roles in the film (compared to only

Spielberg and his wife, Kate Capshaw, went to the former Nazi death camp at Auschwitz before the filming of Schindler's List.

twenty-two in *Jurassic Park),* and 30,000 extras were used. The story spans several years, like *The Color Pur-ple.* For important moments in the film, Spielberg backlit his characters, using the power of light to draw audiences into a scene, the way he had in *E.T.* To build drama, Spielberg "crosscut" between two events happening at

> TO MAKE *SCHINDLER'S LIST,* SPIELBERG NEEDED ALL THE FILMMAKING SKILLS HE HAD ACQUIRED DURING HIS TWENTY YEARS AS A DIRECTOR.

the same time. Most of all, Spielberg used the same dramatic themes he had developed in many of his earlier films: rescue from danger; people yearning for the safety of home and family; a man becoming a father figure to people who need him; and a little guy triumphing over wicked, powerful forces.

The filming of *Schindler's List* began in March 1993. Much of the film was shot in Poland, where the story had occurred. One hundred and forty-eight sets were constructed at thirty-five different locations.

Schindler's List was filmed quickly. Many scenes were shot with a handheld camera so that the film would not look too "polished." Scenes of sudden violence were filmed from a distance, as if the camera just happened to see the action. Cameraman Janus Kaminski said the raw look of the film was intentional. The filmmakers hoped that audiences in the future would not know that *Schindler's List* was made fifty years after the Holocaust. To make the film seem even more like a document from World War II, Spielberg decided to use black-and-white film. Only the beginning, the ending, and one special detail were filmed in color. The special detail was a little girl's red coat.

Schindler's List opens with a tiny sound: a match is struck to light candles for the Sabbath. A Jewish family is gathered around a table, singing a song of worship. As the candles burn down, color fades from the scene. When the last candle goes out, the picture becomes black and white.

The quiet scene is shattered by the noise of a locomotive. It is September 1939, and Jews from the countryside are arriving at the train station in Kraków, Poland. The new arrivals call out their names, and officials sitting at small tables type their names onto lists. Throughout the film, Nazi bureaucrats make lists of Jews who are to be rounded up, moved into walled-off ghettos, shipped to concentration camps, and killed.

Oskar Schindler, a German businessman from Czechoslovakia, has moved to Kraków to make his fortune. He contracts with the Nazi officials to use Polish Jews as slave laborers in his enamelware factory. He even gets the Jews themselves to finance the factory. But Schindler treats his workers as fairly as the Nazis will allow. He feeds his workers well and pays them in valuable pots and pans. Word spreads among the Jews that Schindler's factory is a haven of safety from the brutal Nazi regime. "They say that no one dies here," a woman says to Schindler. "They say that you are good."

Schindler uses all his charm and his skill at "presentation" to win orders for his factory and to persuade the

Nazis to keep their hands off his workers. A timid, puzzled accountant named Itzhak Stern runs Schindler's business for him. Only gradually does Stern come to believe that Schindler is more than just a greedy businessman. Even Schindler himself sometimes seems surprised at his own concern for his workers.

In 1942 a Nazi officer named Amon Goeth comes to Kraków to empty the ghetto. Under Goeth's command, the Jews are rounded up and taken to a labor camp. Those who resist and those who cannot work are shot. Schindler watches the destruction of the ghetto from a hillside above the town. Amid the shouting and the shooting, one figure captures Schindler's attention—a little girl wearing a red coat. Later Schindler sees that red coat after the Nazis have killed the girl and thrown her into a giant pit of corpses.

Amon Goeth is a drunken, flabby killer who likes to sit bare-chested on his balcony and shoot Jews in the labor camp below his villa. Schindler becomes friends with Goeth, forcing down the revulsion he feels for the commandant. He persuades Goeth to let the Schindler workers leave the camp each day to come to the enamelware factory, where they can be fed and cared for. When Goeth is ordered to close the labor camp and ship all the remaining Jews to Auschwitz, Schindler offers Goeth an enormous bribe. He will pay Goeth to let him take nearly 1,200 Jews to a new factory in Czechoslovakia.

Itzhak Stern types a list of every Jew who works for Schindler. Stern is overwhelmed by Schindler's brave and generous act. When he is done, he holds up the list. "The list is an absolute good," Stern tells Schindler. "The list is life."

"The list is an absolute good. The list is life."

Schindler's male workers are transported safely to Czechoslovakia, but the women are mistakenly sent to Auschwitz. As Schindler rushes to their rescue, the women are stripped naked and herded into a shower room. They have heard that the showers at Auschwitz spray poison gas, but this day the showers spray water. The women are spared, and before they can be gassed by the Nazis, Schindler arrives to take them to his factory. There the "Schindler Jews" spend the remainder of the war in safety.

When peace returns, Schindler prepares to leave the factory. His workers gather around him and present him with a gold ring that they have made. The inscription on the ring is a saying from the Talmud, written in Hebrew. Itzhak Stern translates it for Schindler: "Whoever saves one life saves the world entire."

At the end of the film, the image returns to color and we see the real-life Schindler Jews with their children and grandchildren. A subtitle tells us that "There are fewer than four hundred Jews left alive in Poland today. There are six thousand descendants of the Schindler Jews." Along with the actors who played them in the movie, the Schindler Jews approach the gravesite of Oskar Schindler, who is buried in Israel, where he was declared "a righteous gentile." As they move past his grave, each of the Schindler Jews places a stone on the burial marker. Placing stones on a gravesite is a very old Jewish tradition. It is a way of making sure that the deceased's memory is not swept away by the winds of time.

In 1994 Spielberg received the Chaim Weizmann Philanthropic Leadership Award.

CHAPTER NINE

A Boy Flying
Past the Moon

Spielberg used his profits from *Schindler's List* to start the Survivors of the Shoah Visual History Foundation. *Shoah* is the Hebrew word for Holocaust. Through the foundation, hundreds of Holocaust survivors have been given the chance to tell their stories on videotape. Photographs and other documents are also videotaped. All the tapes become part of a multimedia database that students can access through personal computers.

Spielberg calls the Visual History project "a race against time." Most of the Holocaust survivors are sixty, seventy, even eighty years old. Spielberg feels it is important to record their stories before they are gone. Then the stories can be handed down to young people. Through the Visual History Foundation, memories of the Holocaust will be kept alive as a tribute to the survivors and a warning to future generations.

In 1994, Spielberg received the Chaim Weizmann Philanthropic Leadership Award. At the award banquet, Spielberg's old mentor, Sidney Sheinberg, said, "Someday Steven might be remembered as much for his efforts on behalf of the welfare of society as for his movies."

Schindler's List was Spielberg's most highly praised film. Almost everyone thought it was a gripping movie and a serious work of art. One of the few dissenters was J. Hoberman, film critic for the New York *Village Voice.* Hoberman complained that in filming the Holocaust, Spielberg had made "a feel-good entertainment about the ultimate feel-bad experience of the 20th century." The most serious topic of modern times, the slaughter of an entire group of people, had been "Spielbergized."

In a way, Hoberman was right. Spielberg could not help bringing a glimmer of hope to the terrible story of the Holocaust. Other critics rallied to his defense, however, and so did audiences. Universal had not expected to make a lot of money with *Schindler's List,* but viewers flocked to it. Word soon spread: this was a film to see.

Each spring, the Academy of Motion Picture Arts and Sciences presents awards to the top films of the previous year. Everyone in the movie business votes to select the year's best movie, director, performers, and other film artists. Prior to *Schindler's List,* Steven Spielberg had never won an Academy Award.

Spielberg had always felt that the audiences were his "real bosses," the people who determined if he had done his job well. But Spielberg still yearned for recognition from his peers, from other filmmakers like himself. He had won awards from the Directors Guild of America (for *The Color Purple*) and from the Academy itself, which had given him the 1986 Irving Thalberg Memorial Award for his special contributions to the film industry. The biggest Academy Awards, however, for Best Picture and Best Director, had eluded him.

Five of Spielberg's films had been nominated for major Academy Awards. *Jaws* and *The Color Purple* were nominated for Best Picture. *Close Encounters of the Third Kind* was nominated for Best Director. *Raiders of the Lost Ark* and *E.T.* were nominated for both Best Picture and Best Director. None of the films had won. The actor-director Clint Eastwood suggested that perhaps Spielberg's early success had made other filmmakers so jealous that they were reluctant to give him any honors.

"I think Hollywood will forgive me once I'm fifty-five," Spielberg said. "I don't know *what* they'll forgive me for, but they'll forgive me when I'm fifty-five." When he made *Schindler's List,* he was forty-seven years old.

On the night of the 1994 Academy Awards, Steven Spielberg, flanked by his wife and his mother, received the long-overdue recognition of his colleagues. *Schindler's List* won the Academy Award as the best film of the year. Spielberg was selected Best Director. Holding his award, Spielberg said, "This is the biggest drink of water after the longest drought of my life."

Over the years, Spielberg has become a Hollywood "mogul." He has wealth and power. He has his own office

"This is the biggest drink of water after the longest drought in my life."

Spielberg celebrates his Oscar wins with his mother and wife.

building, built by Universal Studios to house Amblin Entertainment. The Amblin office complex includes a game room, movie theater, kitchen, gymnasium, fish pond, and vegetable garden. As a mogul, Spielberg can make any film he wants, and he can use his influence to help other young filmmakers get started. His most famous protégé is Robert Zemeckis, the director of *Back to the Future, Who Framed Roger Rabbit, Forrest Gump,* and *Contact.*

As a producer, Spielberg provides the money and organization to help other filmmakers. He loves stories that

Director Robert Zemeckis is one of Spielberg's protégés.

appeal to "the kid in all of us," and he likes to help other directors put those stories on film. Richard Donner directed *The Goonies,* a film that Spielberg produced from a story he had written. "Steven is over your shoulder the whole time," Donner said. "He always bows to you because you're the director, but he's got so many good ideas that you want to grab every one of them."

Spielberg acted as executive producer on the animated Fievel films (*An American Tail* and *Fievel Goes West*), the *Back to the Future* series, the two *Gremlins* films, *Men in Black* and many others. Spielberg probably will continue to be what one critic called him, "the General Motors of kids' movies."

In addition to movies, Spielberg has helped to produce several popular television shows, including *ER,* the long-running series about emergency-room doctors. Developed by Spielberg and *Jurassic Park* author Michael Crichton, *ER* quickly became the top-rated show on television.

With so much power and responsibility, it would have been easy for Spielberg to give up directing and simply run his company. That is what George Lucas decided to do after directing *Star Wars.* Lucas felt he could no longer "express himself" as a director, and making big-budget movies had become too difficult. He had to deal with huge budgets, thousands of people, complicated equipment, and locations all around the world. To maintain control over the many aspects of his films, Lucas became a producer. He left the job of directing to others.

Spielberg was not willing to give up his position as director. A producer makes a film happen, but a director makes it art. Spielberg has always considered himself an artist. More than anything, he wants to give life to the images and stories he sees in his imagination. In 1985 Spielberg said, "Yeah, I'm a mogul now. And I love work the way Patton loved the stink of battle. But when I grow up I still want to be a director."

Spielberg's business partner, Jeffrey Katzenberg, commented on how family life has mellowed Spielberg. Movies no longer consume every moment of Spielberg's day. "I perfectly understand the ground rules," Katzenberg

The "dream team": Jeffrey Katzenberg, Steven Spielberg, and David Geffen.

said. "8:30 to 5:30, Monday to Friday, is mine. Everything else is Kate's."

In October 1994, Spielberg did something that few film-makers have ever been able to do successfully. He started his own movie studio. In the whole history of Hollywood, there have been only ten major studios. Paramount, Universal, Twentieth Century-Fox, United Artists, Metro-Goldwyn-Mayer, Warner Brothers, and Columbia are the oldest major studios. Disney is an old studio that became "major" during the last twenty years. Only two new studios, TriStar and Orion, were started in the past seventy years, and one of those (Orion) went bankrupt. Spielberg decided to gamble part of his $600-million personal fortune on the success of a new studio.

To launch the new studio, Spielberg formed a partnership with two other Hollywood moguls, Jeffrey Katzenberg and David Geffen. Katzenberg is the former head of production at Walt Disney Studios. He helped build Disney into the most powerful studio in Hollywood by turning out animated films like *Beauty and the Beast, Aladdin,* and *The Lion King.* Katzenberg and Spielberg worked together on the production of *Who Framed Roger Rabbit,* and they are partners in a Los Angeles restaurant called DIVE!

David Geffen began his career as a music producer, building his own company, Geffen Records, which he sold for a fortune. He also has produced several movies, including *Beetlejuice* and *Interview with the Vampire.*

At the news conference announcing the new studio, Jeffrey Katzenberg gave the partners a name that stuck. "This has got to be a 'dream team,'" said Katzenberg. "Certainly it's my dream." Newspaper reporters began calling the partners "the Dream Team." When it came time to pick a name for the new studio, Spielberg suggested they call it DreamWorks. Katzenberg and Geffen agreed.

DreamWorks SKG (*SKG* for *S*pielberg *K*atzenberg *G*effen) produces movies, animated films, television shows, music, and multimedia software. "We're interested in creating a company that will outlive us all," Spielberg said.

The new company quickly formed an alliance with Bill
Gates, the president of Microsoft Corporation, the world's
most important producer of computer software. With Microsoft's participation, DreamWorks Interactive will produce computer games and interactive software.

DreamWorks also signed agreements with ABC television, HBO, and the IBM computer company. George
Lucas agreed to help DreamWorks build a state-of-the-art
facility for digital editing and special effects.

In its first few years, the studio's television and music
efforts did not meet with great success. Its first film,
Peacemaker, an action thriller, got only a mediocre recep-
tion from audiences, as did *Amistad,* the first film that
Spielberg directed for the studio. *Amistad* is the story of
an 1839 slave rebellion aboard a Spanish ship. The slave
ship lands in the United States, where ex-president John
Quincy Adams comes out of retirement to represent the
slaves in court. With his help, the Africans are granted
freedom and return to Sierra Leone, their home.

It was only a matter of time before DreamWorks re-
bounded at the box office. In 1998, the studio had a huge
year with the successes of *Deep Impact, The Prince of
Egypt, Antz,* and especially *Saving Private Ryan.* Dream-
Works co-produced and Spielberg directed this film, a
World War II epic starring Tom Hanks, with Paramount
Pictures Corporation. Beginning with a gripping 20-
minute combat scene that was praised as the most realistic portrayal of battle ever filmed, *Saving Private Ryan*
follows a small group of soldiers who must rescue a

Spielberg gives some pointers to actors in full World War II combat gear during the filming of 1998's Saving Private Ryan.

paratrooper, the last survivor of five brothers sent to fight in Europe, from behind enemy lines. They are acting on orders direct from the Army's chief of staff, who fears that the news of five brothers dying in the war will sap morale back in the United States.

Spielberg received an Oscar for Best Director for Saving Private Ryan *at the 71st Annual Academy Awards in Los Angeles.*

Saving Private Ryan won five Oscars, including one for Spielberg as best director. Spielberg and Tom Hanks also received the highest honor given to civilians by the U.S. Navy, the Distinguished Public Service Award, for helping young officers and sailors to better understand how to serve their country. With *Saving Private Ryan,* Spielberg had proved once again that he was capable of making serious and powerful movies.

1999's *American Beauty* was another hit for Dream-Works that won big at the Academy Awards. The film was awarded five Oscars, including the award for best picture. At the Oscar ceremonies, Spielberg presented the best director award to *American Beauty* director Sam Mendes, who thanked Spielberg for handing him the script. And the film's producers gave thanks to Dream-

Works and particularly Spielberg for giving them the freedom to make the movie, a dark, disturbing comedy about the disintegration of a suburban family.

With these recent successes, DreamWorks appears to be living up to its potential to become a major studio. In addition, Spielberg has allied his Amblin label to DreamWorks, which will lend prestige to the studio's future films.

Over the years, the Amblin logo has become familiar to audiences all around the world. It tells audiences that a film or television program was directed by Steven Spielberg or produced by his company. The logo includes the famous image from the movie *E.T.*—the outline of a boy riding a bicycle across the moon. It is an image that seems to capture the spirit of Steven Spielberg and his remarkable career. The boy, like Steven Spielberg, has had the courage to live his dreams. "I don't dream at night that much," Spielberg once said, "because I dream all day. I dream for a living."

FILMOGRAPHY

Motion pictures directed by Steven Spielberg:

Duel (1971)

The Sugarland Express (1974)

Jaws (1975)

Close Encounters of the Third Kind (1977)

1941 (1979)

Raiders of the Lost Ark (1981)

E.T. The Extra-Terrestrial (1982)

Twilight Zone—The Movie, "Kick the Can" segment (1983)

Indiana Jones and the Temple of Doom (1984)

The Color Purple (1985)

Empire of the Sun (1987)

Indiana Jones and the Last Crusade (1989)

Always (1989)

Hook (1991)

Jurassic Park (1993)

Schindler's List (1993)

The Lost World: Jurassic Park (1997)

Amistad (1997)

Saving Private Ryan (1998)

The Unfinished Journey (1999)

A.I. (2001)

Minority Report (2001)

S O U R C E S

9 Douglas Brode, *The Films of Steven Spielberg* (New York: Citadel Press, 1995), 235.
10 Ibid.
16 Philip M. Taylor, *Steven Spielberg: The Man, His Movies and Their Meaning* (New York: Continuum Publishing Co., 1992), 58.
17 Ibid., 51.
17 Ibid., 45.
17 Ibid., 22.
18 Ibid., 54.
20 Rosanne Keynan, "Spielberg Leads Huge Holocaust On-Line Project," *Los Angeles Times* (Oct. 1, 1994), B4.
21 Denise Worrell, *Icons: Intimate Portraits* (New York: Atlantic Monthly Press, 1989), 39–40.
27 Brode, *The Films of Steven Spielberg,* 18.
28 Taylor, *Steven Spielberg: The Man, His Movies and Their Meaning,* 62.
30 Ibid., 50.
37 Brode, *The Films of Steven Spielberg,* 53.
37 Nancy Griffin, "In the Grip of Jaws," *Premiere* (October 1995), 88.
43 Taylor, *Steven Spielberg: The Man, His Movies and Their Meaning,* 63.
43 Jeanine Basinger, *American Cinema* (New York: Rizzoli, 1994), 263.

43 Dale Pollock, *Skywalking: The Life and Films of George Lucas* (Hollywood, Calif.: Samuel French, 1990), 68–69.
45 Ibid., 118–119.
46 Taylor, *Steven Spielberg: The Man, His Movies and Their Meaning,* 16.
51 Tony Crawley, *The Steven Spielberg Story: The Man Behind the Movies* (New York: Quill Press, 1983), 85.
64 Brode, *The Films of Steven Spielberg,* 22.
64 Ibid., 24.
67 Ibid., 162.
72 Ibid., 148.
75 Ibid., 172.
79 James Brady, "In Step With: Kate Capshaw," *Parade Magazine* (Jan. 7, 1996), 16.
80 Elaine Dutka, "On Filmdom's A-List of a Lifetime," *Los Angeles Times* (March 4, 1995), F1.
80 Ibid., F14.
83 Don Shay and Jody Duncan, *The Making of Jurassic Park* (New York: Ballantine Books, 1993), 56.
86 Ibid., 43.
86 Ibid., 85.
86 James Brady, "In Step With: Laura Dern," *Parade Magazine* (Oct. 23, 1994), 26.
88 Ibid.

90 Don Shay and Jody Duncan,
    *The Making of Jurassic
    Park,* 89.

91 Ibid., 68.

94 Brode, *The Films of Steven
    Spielberg,* 233.

94 Elaine Dutka, "On
    Filmdom's A-List of a
    Lifetime," F1.

104 "Spielberg Honored at
    A-List Benefit Event," *Los
    Angeles Times* (Oct. 3,
    1994), E4.

105 Taylor, *Steven Spielberg:
    The Man, His Movies and
    Their Meaning,* 12.

108 Donald R. Mott and Cheryl
    McAllister Saunders, *Steven
    Spielberg* (Boston: Twayne
    Publishers, 1986), 146.

109 Taylor, *Steven Spielberg:
    The Man, His Movies and
    Their Meaning,* 20.

109–110 Richard Corliss, "Hey, Let's
    Put On a Show!" *Time*
    (March 27, 1995), 60.

111 Alan Citron and Claudia
    Eller, "'Dream Team' Trio
    Outline Plans for Studio,"
    Los Angeles Times (Oct. 13,
    1994), A23.

115 Denise Worrell, *Icons:
    Intimate Portraits,* 46.

S E L E C T E D   B I B L I O G R A P H Y

Books

Basinger, Jeanine. *American Cinema.* New York: Rizzoli, 1994.

Brode, Douglas. *The Films of Steven Spielberg.* New York: Citadel Press, 1995.

Chell, David. "Allen Daviau" (interview) in *Moviemakers at Work: Interviews by David Chell.* Redmond, Wash.: Microsoft Press, 1987.

Ebert, Roger, and Gene Siskel. *The Future of the Movies.* Kansas City: Andrews and McNeel, 1991.

Farber, Stephen, and Marc Green. *Outrageous Conduct: Art, Ego, and the Twilight Zone Case.* New York: Arbor House, 1989.

Hargrove, Jim. *Steven Spielberg: Amazing Filmmaker.* Chicago: Childrens Press, 1988.

Keneally, Thomas. *Schindler's List.* New York: Simon & Schuster, 1982.

Kolker, Robert. *A Cinema of Loneliness.* New York: Oxford University Press, 1988.

McKenzie, Alan. *The Harrison Ford Story.* New York: Arbor House, 1984.

Mott, Donald R., and Cheryl McAllister Saunders. *Steven Spielberg.* Boston: Twayne Publishers, 1986.

Pollock, Dale. *Skywalking: The Life and Films of George Lucas.* Hollywood: Samuel French, 1990.

Shay, Don, and Jody Duncan. *The Making of Jurassic Park.*
   New York: Ballantine Books, 1993.

Taylor, Philip M. *Steven Spielberg: The Man, His Movies and
   Their Meaning.* New York: Continuum Publishing
   Company, 1992.

Worrell, Denise. "The Eternal Childhood of Steven Spielberg,"
   in *Icons: Intimate Portraits.* New York: Atlantic Monthly
   Press, 1989.

Articles

Brown, Corie. "Making the Dream Work: Problems and
   Possibilities for a Fledgling Studio." *Newsweek,* July 19,
   1999, 42.

Citron, Alan, and Claudia Eller. "'Dream Team' Trio Outline
   Plans for Studio." *Los Angeles Times,* October 13, 1994, A1.

Dutka, Elaine. "On Filmdom's A-List of a Lifetime." *Los
   Angeles Times,* March 4, 1995, F1.

Ebert, Roger. "Steven Spielberg: the Moviemaker." *Time,* June
   8, 1998, 128.

Griffin, Nancy. "In the Grip of *Jaws.*" *Premiere,* October 1995, 88.

Groves, Martha. "Digital Yoda." *Los Angeles Times,* June 4,
   1995, D1.

Hall, Jane. "'Dream Team,' ABC Plan Joint Venture." *Los
   Angeles Times,* November 29, 1994, A1.

Harmon, Amy. "E.T. Reaches Out." *Los Angeles Times,* June 6, 1995, D2.

Keynan, Rosanne. "Spielberg Leads Huge Holocaust On-Line Project." *Los Angeles Times,* October 1, 1994, B4.

Masters, Kim. "Private Spielberg: The Much-lauded Co-founder of DreamWorks May Be Looking to Do More Work on His Own." *Time,* April 5, 1999, 64.

Rand, T.G. "Bearing Witness to Their Tortured Past." *Los Angeles Times,* February 9, 1995, E10.

Smith, Dinita. "It's . . . ! Liam Neeson." *The New York Times Magazine,* December 4, 1994, 69–71.

Weinraub, Bernard, and Mark Giberson. "'Dream Team' Pools Talent, Clout in an Imagination-Stirring Merger." *Pasadena Star News,* October 13, 1994, A1.

INDEX

*Steven Spielberg and George Lucas put their handprints in the
cement in Hollywood's "Walk of Fame" in 1984.*

P H O T O   A C K N O W L E D G M E N T S

Photographs are used with permission of: AP/Wide World Photos,
pp. 2, 51, 54, 65; Universal City Studios Inc., courtesy of MCA
Publishing Rights, a division of MCA Inc., pp. 6, 36, 39, 48, 66, 95,
100; Archive Photos/Fotos International, pp. 11, 44, 56, 63; Class-
mates.com Yearbook Archives, pp. 12, 18; © Lisa Rose/Globe Photos
Inc., pp. 15 (top), 85; © Ralph Dominguez/Globe Photos Inc., p. 15
(bottom); Hollywood Book and Poster, pp. 22, 34, 42 (top left, top
right), 52; Photofest, pp. 24, 29, 42 (bottom left, bottom right), 68, 73;
© Bettmann/Corbis, pp. 25, 61 (both), 71, 82, 96, 106, 108, 128;
© Michael Ferguson/Globe Photos Inc., p. 27; Globe Photos Inc.,
pp. 47, 89; © David Parker/Globe Photos Inc., pp. 58, 81; © Vincent
Zuffante/Star File Inc., pp. 78, 102; Sega of America, Inc., p. 90;
© Dave Bennett/Globe Photos Inc., p. 92; © J. Mayer/Star File Inc.,
p. 107; Reuters/Sam Mircovitch/Archive Photos, p. 110; © All
Action/Retna Ltd., p. 113; © AFP/Corbis, p. 114.

Front cover photo: © Steve Granitz/Retna Ltd.
Back cover photo: © Andrea Renault/Globe Photos Inc.

ABOUT THE AUTHOR

Tom Powers lives in San Francisco, where he is the editor of *Release Print,* a monthly magazine for independent filmmakers. He has taught courses in film studies, screenwriting, and mass media at leading universities around the country and has published several books for young adults and special education readers. His previous books for Lerner include *Movie Monsters* and *Horror Movies.*

Other paperback editions in the BIOGRAPHY® series:

BILL GATES

BRUCE LEE

THE 14TH DALAI LAMA

GEORGE LUCAS

JESSE VENTURA

JIMI HENDRIX

JOHN GLENN

LATIN SENSATIONS

LEGENDS OF DRACULA

MARK TWAIN

MUHAMMAD ALI

PRINCESS DIANA

ROSIE O'DONNELL

WOMEN OF THE WILD WEST